CELTIC I

Poems and Paintings
by
Rita Stynes Strow

XULON PRESS

Xulon Press
2301 Lucien Way #415
Maitland, FL 32751
407.339.4217
www.xulonpress.com

© 2021 by Rita Stynes Strow

All rights reserved solely by the author. The author guarantees all contents are original and do not infringe upon the legal rights of any other person or work. No part of this book may be reproduced in any form without the permission of the author. The views expressed in this book are not necessarily those of the publisher.

Printed in the United States of America

Paperback ISBN-13: 978-1-6628-0912-5
Ebook ISBN-13: 978-1-6628-0921-7

Rita Stynes Strow was born in Ireland
and was educated there and in London.
She now resides in the Princeton area,
where she paints and writes poetry.

COVER "GRANNIA UAILE"
40 " x 30"
OIL ON CANVAS

Table of Contents

A Fantasy Meeting	9
Mozart's Elvira Madigan	10
Fra Angelico	11
Grief	13
Halloween	14
One Never Knows with June	15
In the Wheat Field	17
In Her Boudoir Under the Banyan Tree	19
May Days Recalled	20
It's Better to Forgive	21
In Helen's Garden	23
Sonnet	24
Summer in the City	25
Ode to Bread	27
November's Here	28
Musings	29
Sonnet – Homage to the Virgin Mother	31
A Dance to Remember	33
An Old Irish Farmer Recounts	34
Perennial Summer Discontent	35
King David's Sorrow	37
Remembering Helen	38
Art in Little Things	39
Ireland 1847	41
Spring Talks	42
The Keen of the Irish Patriots	43
Sonnet for Christ	45
Swallows	46
The Dark Night of Faith	47
Thoughts of Home (Karachi 1965)	49
The Peacock	50
The Soul of the Rose by John William Waterhouse	51
Rosary Beads	53
The Three Types of Love	55
"Thy Beauty is Past Praise"	56
Do You Enjoy What I Enjoy?	57
Angela's Wake	60
Trapped	61

Cephas	62
Concerto	63
My Thoughts on What Holidays Mean	65
What Once Was	66
Where Have All the Memories Gone?	67
The Ground Hog and the Turkey	68
Time	69
Watching	71
On Seeing A Medieval Book of Hours	72
Listening	73
The Rat and the Leprechaun	75
What Is Forever?	76
An Epiphany	77
Where Have All the Words Gone?	79
Little Thing	80
Winter Blues	81
Clouds	83
A Reverie	85
The Mystic's Prayer	86
Decision, Indecision	87
Derrynane	89
An Apostle Remembers	90
Wistful Hoping	91
A Nymph Speaks	93
The Thimble	94
Thoughts About Magic	95
Sounds of the Sea	97
The Final Years	98
Who Am I	99
The Changing Wind	101
Newgrange	102
May Memories	103
A Lasting Memory	105
One Starlit Night	106
Particular Steps	107
Mysterious Sleep	109
Oh God What Have They Done	111
God Is Love	113
A Lesson Learnt	114

List of Paintings

King Lír 8

The Finding 12

Oisín in the Land of Perpetual Youth 16

Queen Maeve 18

Aoife and the Swans 22

At Emmaus 26

Celtic Madonna 30

The Marriage at Cana 32

King David 36

Maeve, Queen of Connaught 40

Christ (After the Book of Kells) 44

The White Madonna 48

Deirdre of the Sorrows 52

The Good Samaritan 54

The Good Shepherd 58

The Holy Family 64

Mary Magdalene 70

The Other Son 74

Martha and Mary 78

The Return of Christ 82

St. Columcille 84

Cosmic Christ 88

St. Bridget 92

The Storm 98

Agnus Dei 100

The Woman at the Well 104

Cuchulainn and Ferdiad 108

St. Patrick and the Paschal Fire 110

Krishna 112

King Lír
38" x 38"
OIL ON CANVAS

A Fantasy Meeting

Can he be lured to spend one hour with me?
Not even in my dreams
can such an event be.
I do have hope that he will beckon me
to sit with him and watch
the genius of his mind
pour out those golden words
that enthrall us for all time.

Maybe, too he will reveal those mysteries,
those unsolved puzzles of his life
that baffle us today.
Centuries have passed
since he played the London stage,
and with his pen created
a world of towering men and women
whose faults and virtues are
woven into every culture,
for glory or shame
immortalizing his name.

Was he a recusant
as some have said,
hiding his faith from Queen and friends?
Was he lonely in those long nights
while he created scenes
of incomparable delight or strife-
far away from Stratford
from his kith and kin?

Would that I might sit down with him!

Mozart's Elvira Madigan

When Mozart played at Versailles
they found his music too sad,
but it is the wrenching sadness
that appeals to me, that shatters
the barrier to eternity:

Elvira Madigan, Piano Concerto in C
number twenty one –
ethereal, profound, a harmony of sound –
notes that fall like jewels over
pebbles in a mountain stream –
that pour the tears of time over
the world's corruption,
and wash the slate clean---
momentarily.

Mozart I am listening to your music
now, which never fails to heal and
turns the agony of life's sorrow
into joy for every morrow.

Fra Angelico

I am in a medieval world
in the monastery of St Mark in Florence
watching a friar paint his brothers' cells.
Nothing can quell his ardor
as he explores the Gospel scenes
with paint and brush
in glowing color.

The virgin wears a lapis lazuli robe
as she bows in humble pose
before the angel's gaze.
He wears vermilion;
his wings are diverse hues –
'tis a fantasy world, yet imbued with truth
and transcendence that transforms
art into religious icons.

This is Fra Angelico,
the humble monk
who wept as he worked
filling Florence with heavenly visions,
and gives us today
a distant mirror
into what once was Christendom.

The Finding
48" x 48"
OIL ON CANVAS

GRIEF

Some say that consolations can be found
in memories shared of the one who died.
I do not find it so.

Some say that touching jewels bestowed
or gifts once given
can help assuage the pain.
I do not find it so.

Some say that only time can heal
the wound of loss.
I do not find it so.

The dull ache will never go,
no matter how much life is lived -
the emptiness cannot be filled.

HALLOWEEN

The eve of all saints
is a glimpse back in time
to the West's ancient culture.
And for a time this evening
we suspend belief in a secular world.

We see strange phantoms
wander the roads again.
The devil is back in fashion,
witches and werewolves cavort together.
Ghosts emerge from the graves
of the long since dead
to roam through streets and highways
of a twenty-first century world.

Black cats, crows and all
that is dark and sinister
stir our primordial fear of the unknown
and our terror of death.

Under the guise of fun and fantasy
we laugh it off
with parties and pranks,
with tricks and treats
and make it above all
a children's feast.

Yet this festival never seems to go away,
for despite all the frivolity and caricature
it points to something,
(if we care to see)
to a world beyond our sense of apprehension,
to another dimension,
to a supernatural realm
which is just as real.

One Never Knows with June

Playful June has come to stay,
capricious in her ways.
She loves to flout our expectations
of warm sunny days:
Why are we chilled to the bone
when the sycamores are in full leaf,
or the rain stings our faces while
the roses are lifting theirs
to spread their perfume everywhere?

Then June, chameleon-like, can sweetly cover all
in languid mood of sunny days, cool nights,
fresh breezes to delight,
can show us her rich flora
and revel in long hours of daylight.

June can stumble too,
mistake herself for August and leave us
sweltering in humid heat,
angry at the fleeting days of spring
and a summer that has come too soon.

One never knows with June.

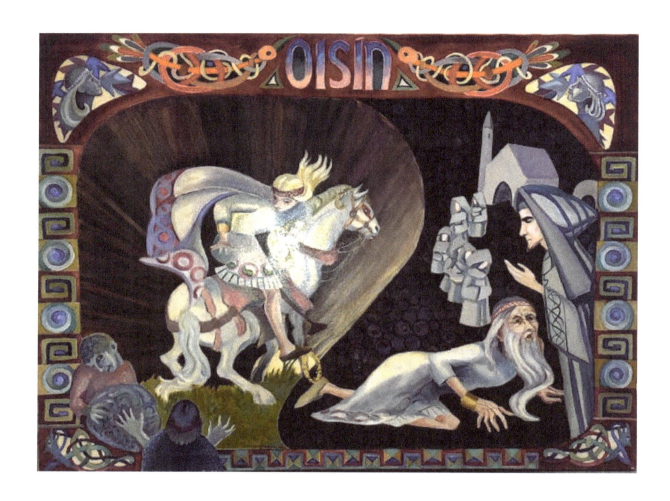

Oisín in the Land of Perpetual Youth
40" x 30"
OIL ON CANVAS

In the Wheat Field

Dancing shadows fall across the waving wheat.
Soon the green stalks will be amber yellow.
Nearby a bird is hiding, shy, discreet.
Something disturbs his reverie,
he flutters upwards on the evening breeze.

The peaceful scene is haunting, hypnotic,
yet changing imperceptibly.
Shadows lengthen, darken, encompassing all.
The field is gone; black night falls.
Without light that bucolic scene vanishes.
A lone screech owl calls.

But above, the night sky
twinkles with a million stars.
I feel safe, God's presence hovers over all.
The Holy Spirit cradles his beloved earth.
The light of day will come again.
My unquiet mind can rest.

Queen Maeve
40" x 30"
OIL ON CANVAS

In Her Boudoir Under the Banyan Tree

Eve sat twirling her tresses
and wondering why she
couldn't eat a certain fruit.
"It makes no sense, such a lovely tree.
Why is that fruit forbidden to me?"

She really knew the answer.
Her friend, the serpent, made it clear:
That fruit, he said, would give her
knowledge and power in every sphere.

"You will be like God," he smiled.
It was an attractive proposition,
"I'm sure Adam will agree."

May Days Recalled

I am nostalgic for the Mays of long ago -
when Summer came on the first day,
and young girls danced around the Maypole,
strewing flowers, singing lyrics,
hoping young men watching
would choose them for a future date –
a hope oftentimes in vain.

May brought Easter season to a close:
on the fiftieth day after came Pentecost,
when the Holy Ghost descended
on the little band of Christians
gathered in the Holy Land.

Whit Sunday people named this festival.
Many went on trips
to fields and forests savoring nature
and lengthening days –
glorying in the bluebells that covered
woodland floors.

May Day changed when it was hailed as Labor Day,
and 'Workers of the World Unite"
became the new refrain.

For some the old meaning remains:
May will always be Our Lady's month-
this at least will not change.

It's Better to Forgive

Forgiveness is the incense that
wafts its way to heaven,
gathering the world in mists of love.
It's hard to free the bonds of hate,
it's easier to capitulate
and seek revenge,

but then a downward spiral begins
and bitterness settles in.
It's better to forgive in haste
than brood in speculation
on an uncertain fate.

It's not a weakness to apologize,
it's a well worth enterprise.
It brings peace to the soul
and deeper inward vision –
it's an action not to be despised.

The Sages teach -
at all times, forgive:
let Mercy temper Justice,
it will never loose its luster.

AOIFE AND THE SWANS
38" x 38"
OIL ON CANVAS

In Helen's Garden

I remember a rose in Helen's garden,
soft, cream-yellow, covered with dew.
Its heart had the glow of an autumn sun setting,
it was drenched when I saw it
with morning dew.
Decades of years have passed since then,
but I remember that rose in her garden so well.
I breathed deep its sweet, rich scent,
and as quickly forgot it
as homeward I went.
God made that rose a perfect thing –
inimitable, lovely - its fragile skin
caressed by wind and rain
as it pumped its perfume to the world.
The clever, artificial roses that I see
have made me remember the yellow rose
in Helen's garden, lovingly.

SONNET

We huddled on the shore that cold June day,
we were four children on our vacation.
The sea was wildly rough, the tide full sway,
we watched in horror what some men dragged in.

A young girl had drowned, her body lay limp;
her parents screamed beside her, grief stricken.
We watched them tie a rag around her mouth.
Shaking, yet staring, we slowly sickened.

No one told us to move away.
We stayed around until the Garda came
and took the poor victim away somewhere.
As children what we had seen caused great pain.

None of us could forget that gruesome sight.
It's engraved in our memories for life.

SUMMER & THE CITY

Summer in the city is hard to take:
boiling concrete streets, a patch of sky,
the burr of air conditioners, the blare of rock
even from subway bands
that seem to ease, but do not,
the stifling feel of metro stations.

Escape? The only resort to keep sane.
But where to go?
Complain, complain;
the beach? Just to get there,
hours of driving, traffic jams,
emotions spiraling out of control,
bickering families, groans, ennui -
at last we reach the sea.

Refreshing? Yes and No.
Too many people, like sardines, on the sand,
too much noise, not a single gull to hear,
drowned out, not by wind or surf
but by what emits from electronic gear,
the modern controversial curse.

But down at the water's edge
looking at the waves
annoyance dissipates.
The calming ebb and flow of
wave after wave
soothes the turmoil in the soul.
There is momentary respite
from the relentless heat and numbing
disappointment of the city's summer season.

At Emmaus
48" x 48"
OIL ON CANVAS

ODE TO BREAD

Golden wheat
caressed by sun and rain,
watched over by the
harvest moon,
readied for the blade.
Under the miller's
sweaty labor
ears morph into
floury mounds.
Callused hands knead
and thrust into
fiery ovens to emerge -
bread;
the crusted loaf,
delicious, wholesome, plain;
food for the folk
in every age.

Hidden in the wheat
a deeper mystery still:
the humble bread
held aloft in the priest's hands -
no longer bread, now
Eucharist,
Symbol,
Reality.
Mystery beyond mysteries
bread becomes
the Deity.

November's Here

There's an ominous look to the sky:
foreboding clouds press down
upon the urban scene
releasing streams of chilly rain.
November's here, I fear.

One might grieve the loss of leaves.
But there's stark beauty in the trees
that now stand bare -
skeleton fingers grasping air.

And the mists that plague the mornings
like smoky fumes that cough and sputter
from old ovens in boiling rooms,
they have a beauty, too.
They carry mystery in their mistiness,
like the pneuma in the matter
of the earth's hard core.

So all is not 'gloom and doom':
for soon we'll hail Thanksgiving Day,
and say a prayer and not despair.
The world is going through travail,
yet far off in the distance –
Spring is on the way.

MUSINGS

Golden apples in a stream,
a hummingbird flies by,
the morning sun lies hidden
in a baby's smile;
the clouds burst asunder
to drench the wilted grass,
I catch a sunbeam in my hand
and surprise; I run so fast.

I do not tease the curled-up cat
or try outrun a hare,
but throw my fishing line
in the silver stream
to find there is nothing there.
The world is so incredible,
but we are not aware --

A riddle now for everyone,
solve it if your dare.
What's hidden in a blade of grass
or in the whistling wind
or lurking near a crescent moon
or dancing by a spring?

Yes, yes, the answer comes,
you guessed it right away.
A myriad of tiny creatures live
who have no thought of us
but spend their days in lovemaking
with the Maker of the Earth.

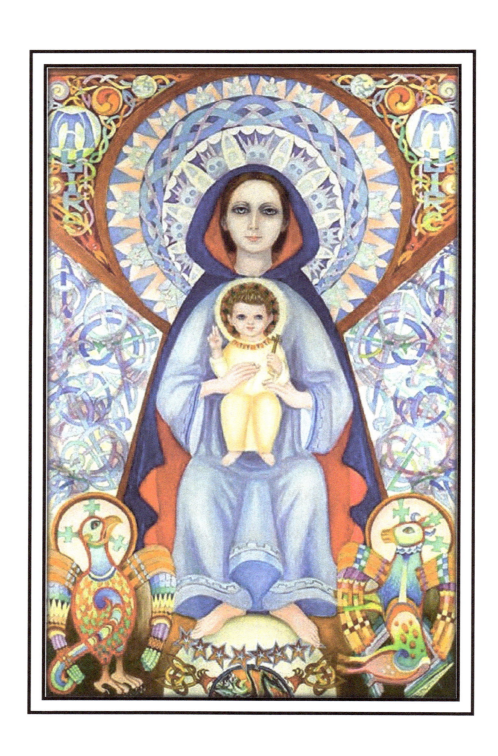

Celtic Madonna
36" x 24"
OIL ON CANVAS

SONNET - HOMAGE TO THE VIRGIN MOTHER

When morning comes reclaiming palest light
The Virgin Mother hastens to the cries
Of struggling children in unending strife.
The world once lovely, now is wretched, dire,
But she is faithful as on Calvary's hill,
Strengthening in anguish all who need her,
All those who will listen, pray and be still.
Will you come lift us, glorious Mother,
Extend our horizons beyond mere dreams.
Bring us to Christ, your sweet Son and lover
To where everything is what it must seem,
No duplicitous words give false cover.

Who understands your greatness? Only faith.
We love you, dearest Mother, keep us safe.

The Marriage at Cana
48" diameter
OIL ON MASONITE

A Dance to Remember

Herodias watched from the aisle
            with cunning smile:
her daughter, center-stage, twisted and swayed
as she danced before the taunting gaze
            of King and Court.
Mesmerized they watched the elf-like grace
            of this genius child
whose bewitching powers could melt a monster
            to a drooling state.
Herod, in his cups, beside himself, cursed and swore
            and spluttered to the whore,
"Whatever, Child, you ask I'll give you,
            though it be half my Kingdom."
The Mother smiled in the aisle:
Salome had won the day.
it only remained for the knife and platter
            to finally end the matter.

An Old Irish Farmer Recounts

There is a place of mystery
on a hill near my old home.
People call it the fairy fort,
I like to go there alone.
The grass is never cut at all;
it grows wild, untamed, until it falls.
The hawthorn trees stand guardian,
for no stranger should go there alone.

On a night when the moon is full
and the earth smells fragrant, sweet
the fairy folk come out and dance
and tap with their tiny feet.
They make music on their pipes and bells
and sing low, rich songs.
The fort is full of wonderment
on nights such as these,
time goes by so quickly,
it almost doesn't seem real.

I've lived here eighty years or more
and now I must confess,
I never really saw these fairy folk,
but the tradition that they live here
is older than my old cloak.

Perennial Summer Discontent

When I was young in my native city,
long hours of daylight passed
curled up in the shade of a tree
reading of other places -
that was summer for me.

But out of Dublin was another theme;
more congenial – a happier scene:
the fragrant smell of new-mown hay,
wild roses, meadow - sweet,
a medley of wild flowers –
this summer feast saturated my mind
with such indelible force that to this day
I can smell again the perfumes,
pungent, lovely, sweet.

And yet I wanted more, much more –
sunlight, heat, the beach where
one could swim without constraint
where temperature mattered not a whit
for warmth would always prevail.

At home white beaches stretched for miles
deserted, flayed by the bullying breezes.
The fields were very green,
but there was a price to pay:
relentless rain limiting our precious play.

But now today I would I had it all again.
I'd trade the heat, humidity, crowded shores,
the traffic jams, the raucous roar of rock 'n roll
for those halcyon days of yore.

But would I be satiated, really?
Possibly yes, possibly no.

KING DAVID
48" x 32"
OIL ON CANVAS

KING DAVID'S SORROW

King David comes alive in Scripture –
a man, brilliant, charismatic, frail
in his carnal nature, yet great in ways
so startling one can only exclaim
and hail this man 'after God's heart' -
one of the greatest Old Testament saints.

I imagine him now looking
as Bathsheba bathes,
his conscience torn but lust too great
controls him.
But then I see him prostrate at his son's death
and see the sorrow for his sin endured;
his love of God consumes him,
it melts God's heart;
henceforth his life will never be the same.

Will I too be changed
when all my sins exposed
cry out for God's forgiveness?
Will my faith endure
the wrenching of my soul?
The secular world today
will call such sentiments theatrics,
for with God's rejection
discernment has fled,
and truth lies scattered in shreds.

Remembering Helen

I often think of you, dear friend
of my early years;
and wonder where you are
though unseen to this world?
We both struggled to know and
fathom life's meaning
so long ago.

"It's strange this accident of birth,"
Helen would say, "Why were we given
this gender, born into this time and place,
into families that seemed great
in many ways, but were flawed and strange;
the epitome of mediocrity,
were they not?
But we loved them just the same."

Our Church taught us early
we were all sinners,
in spite of that our destiny was great.
Whereas you my good friend
have reached your telos long before me,
I continue on my earthly way.

I can only imagine
the joy that surrounds you,
and you must know now
the answers to our great debates.
One day, as yet unknown,
I will join you in the great hymn of praise.

ART IN LITTLE THINGS

'Tis said that when Mozart dined alone
he set his table with great care,
with candles, flowers if possible,
and silver ware.

Why did he bother? Not me,
I make no rituals for drinking tea.
Yet, I do believe
small gestures done with art
can bring beauty to the heart
of an ugly world.

But will people make the effort anymore?
It's easier to ignore the rose,
than bask in its beauty
and watch its petals unfold.

MAEVE, QUEEN OF CONNAUGHT
40" x 30"
OIL ON CANVAS

IRELAND 1847

What was childhood like that time long ago?
When ghostly famine stalked our lovely land.
Little ones cried out for their potatoes.

Blight destroyed the only food folk could grow,
For John Bull kept the wheat crop for himself.
What was childhood like that time long ago?

Parents in agony lost their control.
They could give no comfort to the dying.
Little ones cried out for their potatoes.

The London bureaucrats were the real foe,
They cared not a whit for the suffering souls.
What was childhood like that time long ago?

A million children died in abject woe,
Millions more were banished to distant shores.
Little ones cried out for their potatoes.

Some apologies came, but oh, so slow.
Can one forgive that monstrous genocide?
What was childhood like that time long ago?
Little ones cried out for their potatoes.

Spring Talks

I've been lurking in the shadows
waiting my moment to burst out anew –
And watch all your grumbling faces turn to smiles.
I've outmaneuvered that hoary one,
Frigid winter.

He stayed on too long.
But now I've come
with all my blessings and warm cheer.
The daffodils will bloom again,
the tulips and the snowdrops
will nod their heads with joy.

You will revel in the beauty
of flowering trees and in the smallest leaf;
in myriad new signs of life
and days of longer light.

I was gone so long
you might have feared my demise.
But now I'm here once more,
and
I'm alive!

The Keen of the Irish Patriots
(Executed Easter 1916)

We hear their voices over Dublin Bay -
faint whispers from a distant past.
What do their voices say?

They ask that you may pay
respect for the sacrifice they gave.
We hear their voices over Dublin Bay.

Even from oh, so far away
their noble lives in stark relief cry out.
What do their voices say?

"Freedom is the hope, the only way
to give our people light and life."
We hear their voices over Dublin Bay.

"Beware, the world's insidious sway
may blind you to forget us."
What do their voices say?

We will remember your plaintive lay -
you did not die in vain.
We hear their voices over Dublin Bay.
What do their voices say?

CHRIST (AFTER THE BOOK OF KELLS)
36" x 24"
OIL ON CANVAS

SONNET FOR CHRIST

To the One who will stride the clouds at His coming
who erstwhile suffered a death of shame,
who walked the hills and valleys shunning
no one, neither leper nor slave; His fame
went before Him – this magnet for men;
His words mulled over for centuries to come,
provoking, debating, condemning over and over again;
He would be loved or rejected through the ages by some;
Christ, towering genius, I salute you,
apogee of the chosen race.
Your arms extend to the long queue
that down the ages sought your face.
Your Incarnation has touched our world forever,
has influenced every thought, every endeavor.

Swallows

The swallows are restless as they ready for flight;
the warmer south world beckons –
it is time to go.
I will miss their constant coming and going
in and out of the barn.
The young ones are grown now;
they will go too.

Will they remember the cool land
where they were hatched?
I think they will:
for in April swallows always come north
bringing the summer in –
such as it is-
with its showers and sun.

They'll have their place as usual in the barn.
As long as I'm alive
they'll come to no harm.

THE DARK NIGHT OF FAITH

Why, when we most believe is it hardest?
the spirit's light contracts, or so it seems,
there is no feeling left,
no tears to moist the soul.
All is arid, consolations flown.
God has withdrawn
and leaves us to our own devices.
But what are these without His care -
vain searching, endless complaining, forever
skimming the surface of deepest prayer,
regrets and anger for all the falls
that have so warped the gift of life;
we are soiled – all.

But where is Hope? This is not all there is.
Search the clouds, the night sky,
the whistling wind,
the toil-worn faces, the little fires
that glimmer here and there
in every humble soul.
Something is alive; a light shines
in the darkest space.
Faith glows, it has not died –
just withdrawn into the shadows.
We are not alone.
From the depths we cry –
our essence will survive.
Slowly, surely, we are guided home.

THE WHITE MADONNA
47" x 23"
OIL ON CANVAS

THOUGHTS OF HOME (KARACHI 1965)

A formless moon tonight,
not round, not crescent - yet
sending light down on this desert;
lighting my face as I sit here
on the terrace.
And this same moon might light my old room
thousands of miles away.
Perhaps these rays are playing now
with my mother's hair.
Silver with silver, and her old face-
I can almost see it clear,
gentle and kind- with that smile…
Awhile she will nod and doze.
Perhaps this moon will wake you, Mother,
as she comes on tiptoes.

THE PEACOCK

A hundred eyes flashed out and
graced the silver rushes
where the frog and waterfowl furtively hid
from the haughty stare.
A lone butterfly spiraled down, the transparent
crystal of his wings
capturing the sun's rays.

Why is this symbol of Pride and Resurrection
so beautiful?
when uglier forms could measure well
the one and obfuscate the other.
Was it in Eden when it all began,
when sin was traded by sleight of hand,
and beauty's luster harnessed
every whim, and no distinctive form
could absolutely win?

Glorious bird of contradictions,
simile for man's perennial flaw,
yet,
when emblazoned forth in all
your exotic splendor -
you proclaim anew the Risen One.

The Soul of the Rose by John William Waterhouse

She looks a Victorian lady -
with a medieval aura.
Her long neck cranes towards an English rose.
Her demeanor - chaste, yet secretly seductive,
is mirrored in her gentle pose.

Her languid looks and grace,
her Madonna face,
reveal more the artist who painted her -
as he indulged his baroque taste.

He loved this style of womanhood -
he loved her hair, - those auburn tresses,
now bundled up, just waiting
to cascade down her blue muslin dress.

The background buildings hint
of Italy or Southern France.
But the rose is the English climbing rose,
lovely - alluring as the lady's glance.

Who is she? We do not know,
nor does it matter, for she is the fantasy
of the Victorian male - a delicate creature
who never seems to struggle
with the demons of the mind.

No, she remains all sweetness, calmness, carefree -
so remote from what women came to be.

DEIRDRE OF THE SORROWS IN A MOMENT OF JOY
38" x 38"
OIL ON CANVAS

Rosary Beads

He sat in the pew fingering his beads.
Fingers crooked, gnarled, moved slowly
over each bead lovingly.
He mumbled his prayers.
Sometimes he cried aloud
with some inner pain.
Eyebrows were raised,
but he did not see the public stares.

His aged face with a thousand lines
betrayed no irritation.
Shuttered away from earth
his spirit seemed to soar
to somewhere unknown.

"What does he see," folks wondered,
"Who is he talking to?"
No answer came.
The world stays in darkness,
only faith can fathom
the loveliness of rain.

The Good Samaritan
48" diameter
OIL ON MASONITE

THE THREE TYPES OF LOVE

The gentle touch on the cheek,
the glance at the other in the firelight,
a silence filled with passion
that speaks louder than a thousand words;
these are the quiet smiles of Eros,
the passionate love of intimacy
as old as Adam and Eve,
yet ever new and exciting.

Then there is the love between friends:
the love that takes the edge off loneliness,
the cup of coffee shared
or the trip to here and there,
It is not great passion, but
just quiet affection, a mutual enjoyment,
the meeting of kindred souls.
This love of friendship
the Greeks called Philio.

The greatest love is sacrificial, Agape.
It is love that gives the last drop of blood
for the other;
it is the love of the mother who never spares herself;
the patriot that proudly stands
before the firing squad;
the martyr who is hung, drawn and quartered
for his religious faith.
This is love beyond reason
without a shred of gain,
a total self-giving that leaves us amazed.

"THY BEAUTY IS PAST PRAISE"

What is the song of creation,
a hymn of praise from the heart of things.
Every blade of grass,
every flower that lifts its head,
every bird that sings,
every mountain, lake and valley
by their very being give glory to Him.

Yet they cannot know whence
their loveliness comes. For them
no consciousness flows to enlighten;
no knowledge of what they are disturbs.
Only man --angst-ridden, and searching--
can grasp the naked beauty of the world.

Do You Enjoy What I Enjoy?

Rain pouring down
through canopies of leaves
making melodies
on a gentle breeze
is a harmony I can enjoy.
But if the wind is biting cold
and I am frozen to the bone,
rain on leaves is an abysmal keen;
I cannot bear the moan.

I love to watch the starry sky
and gaze into the immensities of space and time
where the haunting beauty of distant lights
twinkle like fireflies of the night.
Yet when I think of what they are -
billions of galaxies,
each with billions of stars -
it's too much, my mind can't grasp.
I search for an answer,
but stop the pursuit-
it is no use.
I relax my mind
and gaze in awe.

To be with kindred souls, friends
who alone know the inner workings of our minds
and can sympathize with failures
and desires is a blessing beyond compare.
But a snare, a snag in the friendship,
some foible, idiosyncrasy,
can destroy the harmony,
shatter the intimacy.

To keep love at its highest pitch
is continuous work,
but a sweet grace
all the same.

THE GOOD SHEPHERD
48" diameter
OIL ON MASONITE

ANGELA'S WAKE

We gathered for a farewell
to the lovely lady on her coffin bed.
Her family were around her
and her many friends.

They talked about her long and fruitful life;
their eulogies were wonderful, sincere.
She lived for joy
and giving in the extreme.

All looked on her corpse where she lay,
the empty shell from what she was;
and looked and stared and
moved with quiet despair.
What horror that she should be there,
this lovely lady on this, her coffin bed–
a nothing now who once was so alive.

Rage, rage at devious death,
that dared claim so vibrant a life.
Yet, in the darkness there
is a gleam of hope,
of light – a ray,
for faith tells us:
death will not have the final say.

SONNET - WILD GEESE

A skein of wild geese dots the evening sky,
Where are they going? I would like to know -
A secret rendezvous? I must not pry.
Perhaps they're fleeing from an unknown foe?
"Oh, just heading south," the lead goose might say,
"Pools and lakes of silver water call us.
Do not interfere, we are on our way."
Who planned their route without a thought or fuss?
What guiding spirit could command them on?
Instinct some say, but no one really knows.
I watch them vanish, soon they will be gone,
Gone to old haunts, I can only suppose.
The sky is empty now; darkness prevails.
The wild goose song is now a distant wail.

TRAPPED

There is a trapped bird
in the grocery store.
He stays at the window,
pathetic, forlorn;
sometimes flying futilely
from wall to wall,
evoking sympathy with his feeble calls.

Can anyone hear him?
Anyone set him free?
Little bird, you have my sympathy,
but I am stymied –
I cannot release you.

What is he dreaming of
as he sits by the window -
beautiful blessed trees,
a nest to care for,
a sky, blue, and vast to soar in?

He will see none of these,
for he is condemned -
a prisoner trapped by forces he cannot control.
Is not the same the world over?
The little bird does not swear,
or tear his feathers out.
He just sits there and stares.

CEPHAS

Don't say a word, I'm trying to remember;
I saw you before; you look so familiar.

I remember now:
You were by the olive tree, gesticulating wildly,
Your weapon flashed in the waning sun.

Now here you are again many months later –
but you look different somehow, I don't know why.
What is it or what has transformed you?

There is a fire in your eye; a spring to your gait,
a calm to your countenance, an indescribable grace.
Some things you say cut to the quick,
yet I am drawn to your words – I cannot resist.

When we came to take Him you did not stay.
I saw you in the darkness slinking away.
Were you a coward then, or just crafty and clever?
Or what did embolden you to change as you did?
'Tis said 'twas the death of the Leader that changed you;
that His words will forever fly in the wind.

CONCERTO

Music augments my moods:
when sadness overwhelms my soul,
Mendelssohn's violin Concerto in E
both soothes and tortures me.
I am drawn heavenward by the reach
of those haunting notes,
like lyrical flames flowing from the Holy Ghost.

How could one person conceive such loveliness
unless he had felt the pain and anguish
of the world of his day.
Yet there is hope - there is relief:
bursts of melodic joy dispel the sadness

In the end there is peace.

I feel empathy with England's queen,
Victoria held Mendelssohn in the highest esteem,
he was her favorite composer.
His music is the stuff of dreams.

THE HOLY FAMILY
48" x 42"
OIL ON MASONITE

My Thoughts On What Holidays Mean

I used to think the holidays
were a touch of heaven.
We rejoiced to honor Christ
and each other.
Christmas, Easter, Pentecost –
the Liturgical cycle became
our holiday cycle -
Family, friends, neighbors celebrated together.

I will forever remember
those halcyon days;
no one questioned the authenticity--
All cultures celebrate their gods:
ancient Celts had Samhain and Lugh;
Hindus, more gods then a few;
Greeks had their Mount Olympus.
Holidays were holy days.

But now I'm not so sure:
the secular world intrudes
to obfuscate the meaning,
the soul of those festivities.

What will be left?
Anemic celebrations.

WHAT ONCE WAS

We stumbled into a rough, untilled field
where thistles, nettles, weeds unseen
made walking hard.
"Why are we here?" the young one asked,
"There's nothing; not even a shack.
I thought you said a house was here."
And so it was; once long ago,
my ancestral home --

I remember it well.
The kitchen was probably on this spot.
Look, these few stones are part of a wall.
I think the hearth was over there.
'Twas many the turf fire I stoked as
I placed the kettle on the hob
while Grandma rocked in her rocking chair,
and crickets sang their evening prayer.

Off the parlor, maybe near this clump
of ragweed, was the secret room,
a priest's hiding hole in Penal times, then
a refuge for my uncles,
on the run from the Brits
in the fight for freedom.

Over two hundred years of one family's life
was lived out in this very place;
now just an overgrown field.

Maybe if I put my ear to the ground
I can hear the sound of long forgotten folk
as they laughed, suffered, lived and died.

There's more than thistles here, young friend.
There's a forgotten world- vibrant- unseen."

WHERE HAVE ALL THE MEMORIES GONE?

I made a list of moments that stood out in my early years
with Dad and me.
Strange there were so few I could count them on one hand;
surely this cannot be.
I lived with this much-loved man for over twenty years,
so where have all the memories gone?

Somewhere in the cerebral cortex of my brain
every memory must be stored.
I just need a type of fishing rod to probe the murky depths
and haul ashore the mundane moments,
the joys, the fears, the countless conversations;
the - what went before; what followed
those precious moments I can recall.

What led up to Father putting cold keys to my neck
when I had nose bleeds?
Where were we going when he took me
on the crossbar of his bike,
and we laughed as the cold wind stung our eyes,
and we could barely shout?
What made me faint when I was eight
and woke up to look into his kind, concerned face?

What happened all the in-betweens of these events?
I wish I had a key to unlock my rusting grey matter,
then I could recollect.
Will it all become clear one day, when we leave our
mortal clay,
and enter the transcendent stage
of forever Now.

The Ground Hog and the Turkey

A Ground Hog was smitten by love at first sight;
He timidly eyed his beloved thrice.
Finally he spoke in a quivering voice,
"Dear Turkey let us be friends forever."
Turkey looked down in mild surprise,
"Ground Hog, you're a foolish fellow.
We are worlds apart, you and I
I'm an intellectual, a PhD;
you're a philistine, practically a nobody."

"Oh, please don't be so harsh with me.
I admire you so – your plumage, your voice so mellow,
your haughty air –
I beg you keep me from despair."

"We-l-l, you do have a handsome coat
and are quite cuddly;
maybe for a little while we could cavort together."
"Oh wonderful, so let's away.
The Ground Hog festival has just begun,
we can have fun before I hibernate."

"Hop on my back, my comical friend,
let's party and stay 'til the end."
So Turkey and Ground Hog flew
off through the woods
and reveled in their friendship
for as long as they could.

TIME

Time flies, be on time, don't waste time.
The clock's the tyrant in our lives,
but on the upside I like the way
it forces us to virtues without compromise;
punctuality, commitment, perseverance.
It's the disciplinarian we try to woo.

Then there's psychological time,
good time, boring time, bad time.
The tick tock of minutes
is not confined to mathematical exactitude;
we squirm, sweat, suffer
some ordeal of the mind –
An hour feels like a lifetime…
is time then a lie?

Time is at the center of our lives.
And of the cosmos, too.
But what is Time?
The measurement of motion?
That's a discarded notion.
The scientists don't really know
what time is, or when
it did begin.

The Big Bang did not begin time
some physicists now say,
they go so far as to maintain
time is an illusion.
It does not exist –
conundrums, conundrums.
In the fifth century, Augustine said it well;
time might be an extension of the mind,
and before the Creation, there was no time.

MARY MAGDALENE
30" x 40"
OIL ON CANVAS

WATCHING

I watched them perching on cables
and flying in and out of the barn.
Their restlessness intrigued me.
But I should have remembered,
they were soon to leave the farm.

It was August in Agher
and the swallows' stay was over -
I had enjoyed them so!
But the southern world beckoned,
their young ones now were grown
and ready to fly.

They will be back in April and
occupy the barn again.
What a marvel
they know when to come and go.
Some say there's a clock
built into their brain,

But who put that clock or instinct there?
No effect without a cause
the philosophers say.
All I know is
the swallows will be back again -
soaring, diving, gliding on gentle breezes,
their scissor-like tails opening and closing –
a constant flutter of movement
making the environs come alive.

When they leave
the place will seem to die.

On Seeing A Medieval Book of Hours

Captivated
by an old Book of Hours under a glass case,
a relic from a past time,
a bolt of inner light pierced my soul.
This little book of prayers
with its colorful illustrations
was handled with enormous care
by generations of a faith-filled line
of noblemen and sires from medieval times.

"Tis a testimony to the Christian faith that was --
to a time when Europe, for all its wars and woes
still looked to the Creator to give Him praise.,
and in tears and anguish begged forgiveness
for sins older than the hills,
and began again and failed.
Yet they never once turned away in loathing
and declared God dead.
It took the false brilliance of a postmodern age
to turn away from the Origin of Life
and end up the world's slave.

LISTENING

When I was young, someone gave me a conch shell:
"Put it to your ear and listen."
I did.
In wonderment, I heard the sea
roar and howl –
as waves crashed on the white shore.
The sound seemed more real
than when I ran and played on the strand.
Did the conch shell tell me more?
Or did I hear more as I listened?

THE OTHER SON
36" x 30"
OIL ON CANVAS

The Rat and the Leprechaun

"You are ugly, - very ugly, indeed,"
said the rat to the leprechaun.
"Really," he replied, "at least I've no fleas
and although I'm old and wizened
I'm quite at ease in my jacket of green
and crimson hose."
"But look at your nose," the rat sneered,
"So long and lumpy, - and heavens, that beard!
It's like the old goat's tethered by the tree."

"Rat, you are insulting. You've no finesse."
The leprechaun descended from his mushroom perch,
"Besides, what can YOU do? –
apart from stealing and gnawing at flesh.
Now, I'm a cobbler: I make the family shoes,
and at midnight when the moon is full
I dance on the green with grace and ease."

"Ha, ha," the rat chuckled, "you don't impress me;
human beings dismiss you, you don't even exist.
They know all about me
and they love me to bits. Just kidding!"

"Rat, let's stop this bickering,
There, let's have a claw, or should I say, paw.
Now you go your way and I'll go mine,
and I assure you, dear Ratty,
for you I won't pine."

So off slunk the rat to his pile of debris,
and the leprechaun went back to his hole near the tree.

What Is Forever?

The butterfly wings its way south
forever flying, fluttering,
flitting from here to there.
The tree forever stands
come winter or spring.
It sheds its leaves, but they return;
this renewal seems forever.
The child of five from day to day
lives in a forever world.

We say – 'would that it were so';
but reality shows its stark face
and reason takes the premier place,
we dare not say - forever.
Nothing lasts;
all is transitory, ephemeral –
life is some moments on a passing stage.
There is no future, only the grave.

But is this written in stone?
Could there not be another dimension-
a mode of being not dreamt of
in average man's philosophy?
Could there not be
a future that is forever?
We must go our way
taking sustenance where we may.

An Epiphany

I sit here in the café eating alone;
other old people sit around munching cakes,
sipping coffee, popping pills.
What, I wonder is in their minds,
do they ever read a thing?

Sometimes they converse, make
fatuous remarks,
their minds seem completely in the dark.
I wonder are they really so devoid of thought?
Am I too harsh on them;
they're really nice, unobtrusive, quiet.
I must get out of here;
must leave this stultifying scene.

Then to my horror I see the truth,
I am one of them, one of these empty minds,
these crippled souls.
What has happened to them, to us?
We have settled down to
bread and circus lives.
I weep, I sigh --
we have ceased to search.

MARTHA AND MARY
48" x 48"
OIL ON CANVAS

WHERE HAVE ALL THE WORDS GONE?

I knew him well, not personally –
his wit was legendary, his plays and poems
were all the stuff of genius…
And yet I could not remember him -
his name that is.
I searched my mind but could only find
his initials –
OW, yes, that was it;
But what did these two letters stand for?

Then a well-known figure came to mind, an actor,
prominent on stage and screen –
Orson Wells?
The initials were correct, the celebrity too,
but this was not the one I sought.
What was my memory doing to me?
I could no longer command it
to recall so simple a thing.

I looked out the window at the falling leaves
once green and vibrant, now dark with decay.
Words, my words were once clear and fresh
but now, are they too falling -
into some abysmal grave in my mind's depth?
Then came a flash of light,
in one nanosecond
he was there, present to me –
Oscar Wilde,
I could remember now.

LITTLE THINGS

That dew drop on the lone rose
catching the rays of late October sun;

That sudden warbling of the mockingbird
imitating the skylark's song;

That cluster of russet mushrooms
growing near the gnarled old elm;

That plaintive bleat of a newborn lamb
taking his first breath of mountain air;

That little boy in innocent wonder
listening to a fairy tale;

That pungent aroma of coffee
brewing on the kitchen stove;

That smiling face; that forgiving grace;
that blessed bonhomie – all thrill me.

The world is really beautiful
when we stop to look.

WINTER BLUES

Drafty winter has come again
with scowling clouds overhead;
it thrusts its icy finger in my ear
and coils around my mind
bringing a dozen fears:

Will I survive if the power fails
and I can't get out
because of winter gales?
Will black ice underfoot
bamboozle me with its bland look?

There might be one bright spot
in this "winter of my discontent" -
the sun could burst through
on newly fallen snow
painting it a golden hue
and for a time obliterate
the drabness I so hate.

I'll wait you out, sharp winter -
forget the boredom
your dark days bring.
Soon you'll be just a memory,
then my heart will sing.

THE RETURN OF CHRIST
48" x 33"
OIL ON CANVAS

CLOUDS

What massive cumulus clouds are in the sky today.
They hardly move; there's not a breath of air.
Are they poised, waiting to be blown away
by the storm that is on its way?

They have such grandeur soaring as they do
with such regal beauty and complexity.
I stop to stare and then I see
a moving world in their immensity.

Images in the clouds appear to come and go,
the animal world is suddenly flitting by –
a dog here, a bird there and on the edge of sky
a jumping cow is crowding out a rabbit and
a snail. It's fun to imagine this menagerie
of shapes and watch how quickly they evaporate.

And then to my mind
the clouds bring another image --
the day that will come towards the end of time -
a day foretold by the Son of Man
when He will come again on the clouds of Heaven
and gather his elect from the four corners of the earth
to reign with Him forever.

St. Columcille
38" x 18"
OIL ON CANVAS

A Reverie

Time will creep up and dreams will end:
I see the swallows from my window
and follow the butterfly as it leaves
the sun-drenched stalk.
I watch a rabbit peek through the marigolds;
look at myriad gnats flutter on a sunbeam
before the lengthening shadows banish them away.

The world will be very beautiful that day.
I will be sad- just a little, maybe.
But memories of love will counteract
my sorrowing mood.
I recall my father's smile at my school success;
my mother's deep concern over some sickness;
the gentle husband who saw no wrong in me;
all the loving hustle and bustle
over the many years.

The sky is darkening now.
I hear the wild geese and the strike of a distant clock.
Voices from the past come racing back—
I let them go.
The wondrous future now unfolds—
Life, the gift so gratuitously given
is being transformed.

I will not be a humming bird in the afterlife,
just a small soul safe in the kingdom
of Christ.

THE MYSTIC'S PRAYER

Somewhere along the edge of time
in some oasis of the mind
the answer came to the mystic's prayer:
he could see it now in all its shades,
this mystery of salvation.

Not many venture to penetrate
the puzzle of time and space,
but for those who do, the blessed few -
the rewards are great and compelling.

True existence is deep within
the human heart
whose search is never ending.

The light of reason points the way
to the mystic's prayer's
fulfillment.

DECISION, INDECISION

I watched a snake slither out
from a hole in the wall,
his head moved quickly from right to left
searching out prey.
Suddenly a hawk swooped down,
the snake in an instant, trapped in his claws,
was whisked away.

The hawk, a marvel of decision,
no hesitation there,
no dithering, vacillating,
no weighing the pros and cons;
the deed accomplished
from the second
the thought conceived.

But,
of course, there was no thought,
just naked instinct.
With reflection comes hesitation.
Much as I would wish to be
as decisive as my swiftly active hawk,
it cannot be.

Instead I flounder like a Hamlet
unable to make up my mind –
whether to wear my hat of green
or crimson hue,
wasting precious time
being the foe
of my own mind.

COSMIC CHRIST
48" diameter
OIL ON MASONITE

DERRYNANE

The white strands of Derrynane
whispered lovingly to me,
Come stay a while and breathe again
the heady salt air; and watch
the restless ribbons of white foam
curl and gently tumble on the purple sand.

I watched the last rays of sun
light on the wing of a lone bird,
as it hovered overhead for one last time
before darkness fell,
engulfing all in nothingness.

Then heavy clouds whirled down
smothering the once tranquil scene
with lashing rains and frightening winds.
This sudden storm morphed rivulets of foam
into thundering waves of violent force.

Did Derrynane whisper to me now?
No, I watched in fear and remembered
the many lives lost here –
the desperate peasants pushing out to sea
in their currachs, foolishly
hoping to smuggle what they could
from frigates of the French Confederates
anchored offshore --
caught in a storm such as this.

Their bodies washed ashore
when all was quiet again.
And the strands of Derrynane
serenely beautiful once more
blew gentle sand
over white, dead faces.

An Apostle Remembers

I was there when the words were spoken.
It was His last supper,

but we didn't know it then.
We sat around the table our hearts full
of fear, and longing,
and anticipation of --
we knew not what.

The night was cold.
The candles on the table flickered.
It was the night before the Pasch.
After we had eaten
He took bread,
blessed it, also the wine.
Then He said those words -

whose depths we cannot fathom,
whose mystery we cannot unravel,
incomprehensible for us then, and
in some ways would be forever.

They were the greatest words
ever uttered on this earth.
To hear them again
I would give my last breath.

WISTFUL HOPING

Watching the sun slowly fade in the West,
the last red feathery clouds
disappear in a purple haze -
the final glorious phase before darkness prevailed,
I sat, feeling sad that this should have to pass.
"Nothing lasts," my sorrow surfaced:
I so wished I could have held this
loveliness forever.

It was the same with so many things:
the visit to my cousin's house
where myself and Brigit sat and talked
for hours and hours, and then –
we had to leave, dragged away by
parents who seemed too busy to care.
"Why do we have to leave?" I grumbled,
but to no avail.
Nothing lasts, my forlorn heart would say.

I sketched some things to hold them longer,
but that did not compensate.
"Nothing lasts," my soul used cry,
"Nothing lasts, except school and chores."
And even these will go.

My solace was in books and prayer
there, at least I could find
people who would quest with me
and together search
for why life has to be.

St. Bridget
48" x 36"
OIL ON CANVAS

A Nymph Speaks

Strange twist of fate that I, the lovely
nymph, Daphne, am now a tree.
It was all Apollo's fault, he chased me to seduce me,
but I would not succumb.
I vowed not to submit to any man.
I wanted to be free to hunt the mountains and woods,
befriend the deer and elves,
to come and go as I pleased.

I did not wish to marry, ever, in spite of Father's plea,
"When will you give me a grandson," he would sigh,
but I just laughed at the silly old dear.
I loved my life until Apollo appeared.
"I am in love with you," he cried –
as if I cared. I just wanted to be free.

I ran from him like a wild thing
but he was swift of foot and soon overtook
my slower pace. He almost caught me by the hair,
I called out to my father, Peneus,
the river-god; he kept me from despair,
and saved me in a unique way –

around my lovely body a tree began to grow,
branches sprung out here and there,
within moments I was no longer Daphne, the fair,
but the laurel tree with victory leaves
of undisputed fame.
Apollo called it his special tree,
but that was little solace for me,
my life was forever changed.

THE THIMBLE

It was so small a thing,
a thimble in a forgotten drawer,
that ushered in a thousand memories
from long ago.

I recall my mother's thimbled finger
pushing her needle back and forth
to weave some woolen strands and camouflage
a hole in a worn-out sock,
or renovate hand-me-down frocks,
brushing tears away as sisters fought
over who got what.

Late into the night she worked
making hats and coats, mending shirts,
patching this and that -
pulling her family through
the terrible times of World War II.

Scarcity, uncertainty stalked the land
would there be a future?
No one knew.
Did respite come with time
and bring relief?
Yes, years before she died
Mother no longer cried.
She could put her thimble away.

Thoughts About Magic

Magic conjures up a world of
wonder, fantasy, dreams;
an escape from reality;
a soothing bewitching of the mind
whimsical, fraudulent,
a refuge from life's monotony;

For a child it could seem real:
a glorious world of what might be.
But magic can be dangerous, too,
if the illusion gets confused with truth.

We end by telling children
there's no such thing as
Santa, elves or leprechauns,
or aliens from outer space -
they're just the figments of
someone's fertile mind.

Reason tells us
magic is a lovely lie,
and in the humdrum of life
we need a little to survive.

THE STORM
30" x 40"
OIL ON CANVAS

SOUNDS OF THE SEA

The many sounds of the ocean
captivate me:
The hypnotic gentle fall of waves
on white sand,
the crashing violence of great sea breakers
against rocks in winter storms;
the lapping song of wavelets
vying with cries of terns and gulls
have all a magnetic pull.

The ocean is a mystery
holding secrets, grim and tragic.
Gazing down into the swirling sea
I see again the day the angry waters
claimed a young girl
who had come to swim
at an Irish seaside resort, Strandhill.
We children watched her body dragged in.
We were not shooed away,
but stood gazing at the dead girl.

I remember listening to the crashing waves
and the anguished wail of a mother.
I can still hear echoes of that day.

The Final Years

No more ambition to torture me, or fear of failure;
I've thrown off those shackles of yesteryear.
Now I can relax and relish without compunction
each comfort, minuscule, mundane:

I can caress with eyes
that lovely rose whose delicate petals
are strewn on the garden floor;
or watch the meandering robin
pick and choose the fattest worm while his mate
warbling among the leaves slyly waits;

see a sunset at Carnegie Lake
glow golden orange, deepen, then mellow
into burnt sienna as the surrounding trees,
and vegetation darken into indigo,
then melt away;

the night sky full of stars,
its restless constellations bewitching, tantalizing
my mind still eager today, to know the why
and wherefore of Nature's secret mysteries.

Comforts abound:
from marmalade on toast
to profound meetings of the mind among friends;
to the sweetest comfort of all –
in the holy place where bell and incense
and ancient chant luxuriate
filling the space
with transcendent Presence
where peace reigns
and fear dissipates.

WHO AM I?

I am the wind in Autumn
gently stirring the maple tree,
loosening the golden leaves
until, one by one they
float to the ground.

I am the wind in Winter
blowing snow in spirals;
freezing lungs and bones
as people flee
from icy cold.

I am the wind that
quietly sings on a starlit night,
brushing the faces of lovers
as they wander hand in hand
on the purple strand.

I am the wind that roars
in anger when hurricanes blow.
My fury wrecks house and home,
for I have nowhere to go
until spent and weary
I slowly die away
to return another day.

Agnus Dei
36" x 24"
OIL ON CANVAS

The Changing Wind

I hear the cry of gulls on the empty beach,
white sand dunes cast long shadows
that sweep down to the strand below.
A chill wind in the air like a banshee moan
penetrates the bone.
It is the homing time for swallows
and for me.

The summer's lethargy is spent,
gone with the fun of former days.
The land is on the cusp of major change:
there is a hint of coming suffering and decay.
Yet I am not loath to leave the humid days
of spring and summer but joy to plunge into
the maze of cool October days.

I love the heady, rich smell of autumn's vegetation:
the heather flush in purple glow,
the fuchsia bursting out in bright carnelian
and the meadow-sweet filling the night air.

O, what if the sun goes down a little sooner –
there are witches and goblins and ghosts galore
to walk the night roads and
stir the soul to think of deeper things:
what follows life, what follows death?
where hope is found in the whispering wind?
in nature's signs and symbols that tell
the seeker who God is?

Newgrange

The shaft of light, morning's first ray
pierces through the rock opening
down the long passage way
to the chieftain's grave.
Some charred bones remain.

The Neolithic man who solved
the riddle of the stars
must have smiled in satisfaction;
the calculations he devised were accurate:

Only on this morning
of the winter solstice
could the wonder have occurred:
the cavern deep inside the mound,
pitch black now luminous
for moments long enough to see
the carvings, script, and sacred grave.

We catch our breath today in awe
at the genius of our species.
From common clay and stone
some ancient engineer hacked out
this marvel to an unknown.

MAY MEMORIES

The flowers of May bring joy and hope
to all the winter-weary folk.
What are these flowers that grace
the streets, the parks, the open fields?
Some names elude me,
but I don't have to know – 'tis
enough to recognize their beauty,
their perennial glow.
Even the weeds that sprout flowers
in out-of-way places
delight the eye and charm the soul.

The flowers of May recall my youth
when we bedecked images
of the Virgin Queen
with garlands of evergreens –
of buttercups, daisies and wild hawkweeds.

These were all we could find
in ditches and hedges:
the loveliest blossoms graced altars and shrines
in churches and wayside places,
for May has always been
Our Lady's special moment.

This custom is honored still
wherever Faith lives - voices sing
to Mary, the Mother of fair Love,
the mystical rose;
the morning star –
this young Jewish girl who
said 'yes' to God
and changed the world
forever.

THE WOMAN AT THE WELL
48" diameter
OIL ON MASONITE

A Lasting Memory

The small room was crowded
as I pushed my way through.
Although it was daytime there seemed
only darkness and gloom.
The flicker of candles threw dancing shadows on the wall,
I remember the aroma of lilies, the silence, the awe.

Moving closer to the bed I could see her,
little Roselie lying there, her pinched face
white as the First Communion dress she wore.
This was my first encounter with death;
I was six years old; Roselie was nine.

We knew her well in the neighborhood,
always in a wheelchair;
"She has a bad heart," her sister would say.
I stared in fear and fascination at the little waxen face;
'What does it mean to be dead?' I tried to grasp.

Her mother broke the silence, speaking without tears:
"Roselie talked to her Daddy before she died,
she called his name and whispered, 'he's coming for me.'
They are both together now."

Suddenly I heard a booming voice
call out my name, "what are you doing here?
Go home this minute."
It was my formidable kindergarten teacher.
She terrified me at the best of times,
but now I could scarcely breathe
for she was right,
I should not have been there.

I had sneaked into that house of mourning
with a group of neighbors unaware.
Now I fled in terror and ran all the way home.
I was filled with fear at what I had seen
and of the teacher who had discovered me.

In time my memory of that teacher faded,
but not the sight of Roselie's dead face.

ONE STARLIT NIGHT

Tonight the sky is ablaze with light;
a festival of stars dazzling, bright;
the landscape of drab houses is cloaked
in blankets of mystery,
woven in misty haze.
Thank God, I do not see their ugliness,
only the sky prevails,
only the sky holds my gaze.
It is everything tonight,
 heaven's gate, the Father's dwelling place.

Are His many mansions reflected in the stars?
My ancestors may be there,
in some mansion outside time and space.
One day I too will be in His dwelling place;
there will be a mansion for me.
I long to dwell in the closest one,
closest to the Father's Son,
the mansion where His greatest lovers are.
Should I dare to hope?
Not if my sins are any gauge.
But my ambition soars above all that;
the greater picture is Christ's undying love
for even those who fail.

Particular Steps

Steps – material steps are everywhere:
they lead to doors, to rooftops, to what you may;
wooden, concrete, old stone, brand new,
or crumbling, overgrown.
All witness to the ebb and flow
of lives that come and go.

Then there are the abstract steps,
vital in debate, in planning;
so necessary to elucidate an argument,
an attack, an addict's efforts
to control his fate.
Steps like these can tyrannize
as they incline to organize to the nth degree.
So they must be thought about carefully.

There are also spiritual steps:
the mystic's way to God;
that Ladder of Perfection whose first rung is –
Divest thyself of self;
shun worldly loves.
These steps are many:
prayer, discipline, self-denial,
a reliance solely on transcendent grace.
Then the summit reached is -
God's embrace.

Cuchulainn and Ferdiad
40" x 30"
OIL ON CANVAS

MYSTERIOUS SLEEP

2 o'clock; 3 o'clock
and still awake!
I am without pain yet
sweet sleep eludes me.

I seek oblivion, but
fear it, too:
Sleep is a little death
the ancients mused -
foreshadowing the
inevitable tomb.

Insomnia makes me
come face to face
with the mystery of being:
for sleep comes with a price:
the soul suspends its inner life;
whither has it fled?

I may toss and turn the night through.
I cannot command sleep;
there is nothing I can do.
Sleep will come only if it choose.

St. Patrick Lights the Paschal Fire
49" x 38"
OIL ON CANVAS

OH GOD WHAT HAVE THEY DONE?

My people, what have you done?
To the Moloch of Modernity
you have offered up the little ones.
They will cry from their graves,
"You took our lives away
when they had barely begun!"

Do you realize what you have done
my Dark Rosaleen?
You voted to kill the unborn,
to wipe them from the face of the earth,
and thereby destroy what was left
of Christian culture.

You held firm through centuries
of war, of misery, of famine.
You held the ancient faith
that Patrick planted.
But now you have tossed it away,

Are you pleased with what you have done,
poor Rosín Dubh?
You are just a nonentity now,
 another blob on Europe's sullied face.

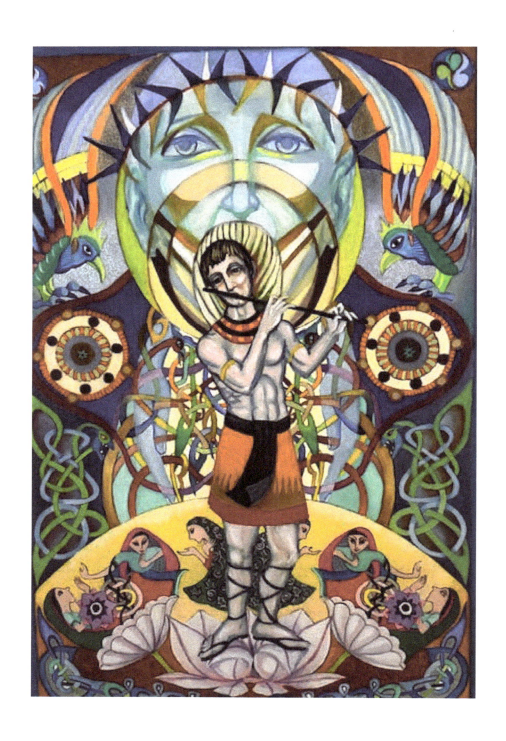

KRISHNA
36" x 24"
OIL ON CANVAS

GOD IS LOVE

Universe upon universe
Tossed and tumbled where He wills:
Our earth is but a meager thing,
Dwarfed by stars, a billion paced
By Him.
His swiftness of thought
Creates immensities beyond our grasp.
He loves – and finds a place to rest
On one small pebble – Earth.
And why?
Because so foolishly He cares
About a race of creatures lit from within
Carrying a spark of Him.
The mind boggles and caves in-
We cannot accept
So scandalous a thing!

A Lesson Learnt

First there's pity:

The sparrow had a broken wing,
'Should I take him home so he can sing
again one day?'
But then the warning came;
do not handle sick or wounded birds,
they can carry diseases
detrimental to human kind.

"Cover your eyes," the elder said,
"So you will not see the
suffering world out there.
Feelings of sorrow can bring you to despair."

Pity is not enough!

Compassion must go further.
It calls for action.
"I must do something for that wounded bird.'
Alas! my hands were tied,
did the world hear my sighs.

"Forget the sparrow's pain," the elder said,
"The greater good demands he cannot,
should not, be saved."

What did I learn from my wounded sparrow?
Compassion needs wisdom to guide
its gaze.

CPSIA information can be obtained
at www.ICGtesting.com
Printed in the USA
BVHW021212090321
602096BV00014B/901